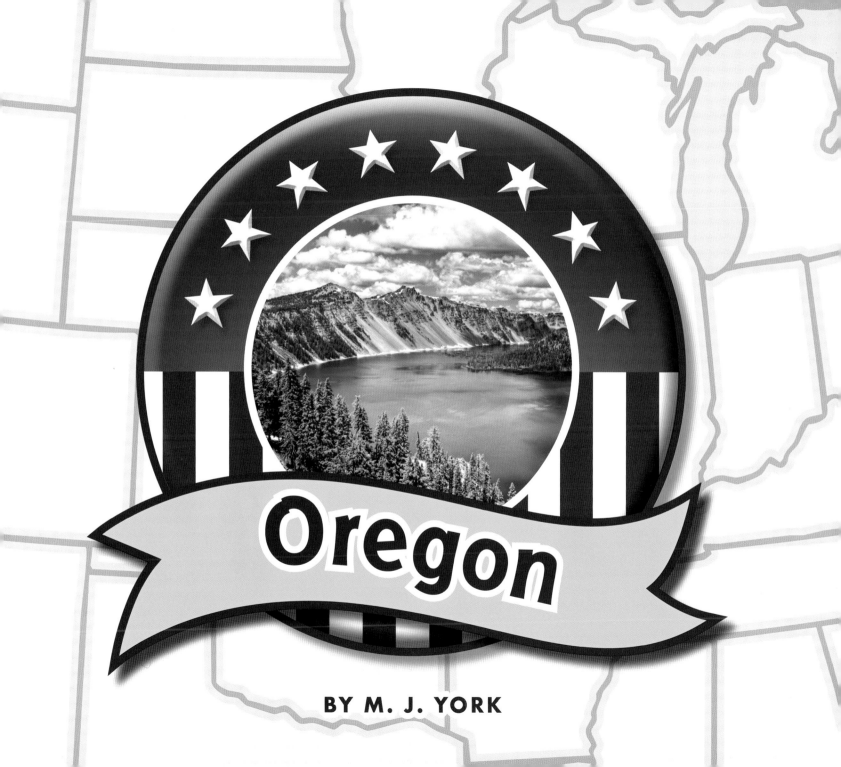

Oregon

BY M. J. YORK

The Child's World

Published by The Child's World®
1980 Lookout Drive • Mankato, MN 56003-1705
800-599-READ • www.childsworld.com

ACKNOWLEDGMENTS
The Child's World®: Mary Berendes, Publishing Director
The Design Lab: Design and production
Red Line Editorial: Editorial direction

PHOTO CREDITS: Lindsay Douglas/Shutterstock Images, cover, 1, 3; Matt Kania/Map Hero, Inc., 4, 5; Bruce Block/iStockphoto, 7; David Birkbeck/iStockphoto, 9; iStockphoto, 10, 13, 17; Lori Howard/Shutterstock Images, 11; North Wind Picture Archives/Photolibrary, 15; AP Images, 19; Horst Heuchlow/iStockphoto, 21; One Mile Up, 22; Quarter-dollar coin image from the United States Mint, 22

LIBRARY OF CONGRESS CATALOGING-IN-PUBLICATION DATA
York, M. J., 1983–
  Oregon / by M.J. York.
      p. cm.
  Includes bibliographical references and index.
  ISBN 978-1-60253-481-0 (library bound : alk. paper)
  1. Oregon—Juvenile literature. I. Title.

F876.3.Y67 2010
979.5—dc22

                              2010019319

Printed in the United States of America in Mankato, Minnesota.
July 2010
F11538

On the cover:
At its widest point, Crater Lake is 6 miles (10 km) across.

CONTENTS

Geography

Let's explore Oregon! Oregon is on the western coast of the United States. The Pacific Ocean is to the west.

WASHINGTON

NORTH
WEST EAST
SOUTH

Columbia River

Astoria

Pendleton

Portland

Tillamook

Mount
Hood

La Grande

Willamette River

OREGON

Pacific Ocean

Salem

Baker
City

IDAHO

Florence

Eugene

Bend

Ontario

Burns

Crater
Lake

Medford

CALIFORNIA

NEVADA

5

Cities

Salem is the capital of Oregon. Portland is the state's largest city. More than 500,000 people live there. Eugene is another well-known city.

Mount Hood can be seen from Portland. ▶

Land

Oregon has a long coast along the Pacific Ocean. The coast has sandy beaches and rocky cliffs. Oregon has mountains, **gorges**, and fast rivers. Two important rivers are the Columbia River and the Willamette River.

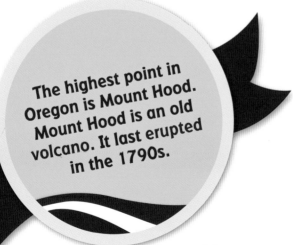

The highest point in Oregon is Mount Hood. Mount Hood is an old volcano. It last erupted in the 1790s.

Many people enjoy camping and boating in the Columbia River Gorge area. ▶

Plants and Animals

The state animal of Oregon is the beaver. The western meadowlark is Oregon's state bird. The state tree is the Douglas fir. It grows in the state's mountain forests.

Oregon's state fruit is the pear. Many farmers in the state grow pears.

The Douglas fir became Oregon's state tree in 1939. ▶

People and Work

Almost 3.8 million people live in Oregon. Some people make computer parts. Some people are farmers. Farmers in Oregon grow wheat and fruit. Others raise cattle. **Logging** is an important job here. People make paper and other wood products. **Manufacturing** and fishing for salmon are also important jobs.

Much of Oregon is covered in forests of Douglas fir and ponderosa pine trees. ▶

History

Native Americans have lived in the Oregon area for thousands of years. They fished, hunted, and gathered food in the forests and rivers. U.S. settlers came to the area in large numbers starting in the 1840s. They traveled in covered wagons. They followed the Oregon Trail from Missouri. Oregon became the thirty-third state on February 14, 1859.

U.S. explorers Meriwether Lewis and William Clark reached the Oregon area and the Pacific Ocean in 1805.

Settlers expanded westward by traveling on the Oregon Trail. ▶

Ways of Life

Many people in Oregon enjoy nature. They walk on the beaches and watch for whales. Some **hike** in the mountains and gorges. Portland is called "the City of Roses." It is home to the **International** Rose Test Garden. Gardeners here breed new kinds of roses.

Visitors enjoy trails and natural areas near Mount Hood. ▶

Famous People

Mel Blanc grew up in Portland, Oregon. He was the voice of Bugs Bunny, Woody the Woodpecker, and other cartoon characters. Matt Groening was born in Oregon. He created *The Simpsons* television show. Children's author Beverly Cleary was also born in Oregon. She wrote the Ramona books.

Cartoonist Matt Groening was born in Portland in 1954. ▶

Famous Places

Tourists visit Oregon to see Crater Lake. This lake is an old volcano. It is the deepest lake in the United States. People come to see Haystack Rock on Cannon Beach.

Haystack Rock towers about 235 feet (72 m) over the beach. ▶

State Symbols

Seal

Oregon's state seal has pictures on it that stand for Oregon and its history. The eagle and the stars stand for the United States. The covered wagon shows how settlers came to the state. Go to childsworld.com/links for a link to Oregon's state Web site, where you can get a firsthand look at the state seal.

Flag

Oregon's state flag has different pictures on the front and back. The front has a part of the state seal. On the back is a beaver.

Quarter

The Oregon state quarter shows Crater Lake. The quarter came out in 2005.

Glossary

erupted (i-RUHP-ted): If a volcano erupted, it released hot ashes and lava. Mount Hood is a volcano in Oregon that last erupted in the 1790s.

gorges (GORJ-iz): Gorges are steep, narrow canyons. Oregon has many gorges.

hike (HYK): To hike is to take a walk in a natural area, such as a hill or a mountain. Some people in Oregon hike in the state's mountains.

international (in-tur-NASH-uh-nul): International means something involving many countries. An international rose garden in Oregon is a popular place to visit.

logging (LOGG-ing): Logging is cutting down trees to use for lumber or other wood products. Logging is an important type of work in Oregon.

manufacturing (man-yuh-FAK-chur-ing): Manufacturing is the task of making items with machines. Many people in Oregon work in manufacturing.

seal (SEEL): A seal is a symbol a state uses for government business. Oregon's seal has eagles and stars to stand for the United States.

symbols (SIM-bulz): Symbols are pictures or things that stand for something else. The seal and flag are Oregon's symbols.

tourists (TOOR-ists): Tourists are people who visit a place (such as a state or country) for fun. Many tourists visit Oregon to enjoy its natural beauty.

volcano (vol-KAY-no): A volcano is a place in the ground, often on top of a mountain, from which lava, steam, and ashes shoot. Crater Lake in Oregon is an old volcano.

Further Information

Books

Keller, Laurie. *The Scrambled States of America*. New York: Henry Holt, 2002.

Labella, Susan. *Oregon*. New York, NY: Children's Press, 2007.

Smith, Marie, and Roland Smith. *B is for Beaver: An Oregon Alphabet*. Chelsea, MI: Sleeping Bear Press, 2003.

Web Sites

Visit our Web site for links about Oregon: *childsworld.com/links*

Note to Parents, Teachers, and Librarians: We routinely verify our Web links to make sure they are safe and active sites. So encourage your readers to check them out!

Index